Scholastic    5/09

**DATE DUE**

| | | | |
|---|---|---|---|
| | | | |
| | | | |
| | | | |
| | | | |
| | | | |
| | | | |
| | | | |
| | | | |
| | | | |
| | | | |
| | | | |
| | | | |
| | | | |

# LIZARDS

## Amy-Jane Beer

**Grolier**
an imprint of

www.scholastic.com/librarypublishing

Published 2008 by Grolier
An imprint of Scholastic Library Publishing
Old Sherman Turnpike, Danbury,
Connecticut 06816

© 2008 Grolier

**For The Brown Reference Group plc**
Project Editor: Jolyon Goddard
Copy-editors: Lesley Ellis, Lisa Hughes,
    Wendy Horobin
Picture Researcher: Clare Newman
Designers: Jeni Child, Lynne Ross,
    Sarah Williams
Managing Editor: Bridget Giles

Volume ISBN-13: 978-0-7172-6238-0
Volume ISBN-10: 0-7172-6238-3

**Library of Congress
Cataloging-in-Publication Data**

Nature's children. Set 1.
    p. cm.
  Includes index.
  ISBN-13: 978-0-7172-8080-3
  ISBN-10: 0-7172-8080-2
  1. Animals--Encyclopedias, Juvenile.
  QL49.N38 2007
  590--dc22

                        2007018358

Printed and bound in China

**PICTURE CREDITS**

**Front Cover:** Creatas.

**Back Cover:** Creatas; Nature PL:
Barry Mansell, Pete Oxford;
Shutterstock: Sim Kay Seng.

**FLPA**: Martin B. Withers 4, 33; **Nature PL**:
Tim MacMillian/John Downer Pro 29, Pete
Oxford 22, Artur Tabor 45, Dave Watts 42;
**Photolibrary.com**: Joe McDonald 30;
**Photos.com**: 14, 18, 26–27; **Shutterstock**:
Anyka 6, EcoPrint 5, Javarman 38, Emin
Kuliyev 10, Steve Lovegrove 2–3, 13, Keith
Naylor 21, Arkadiy Yarmolenko 41; **Still
Pictures**: John Cancalosi 9, 46, James
Gerholdt 37, Hans Pfletschinger 17,
Wolfgang Poelzer 34.

# Contents

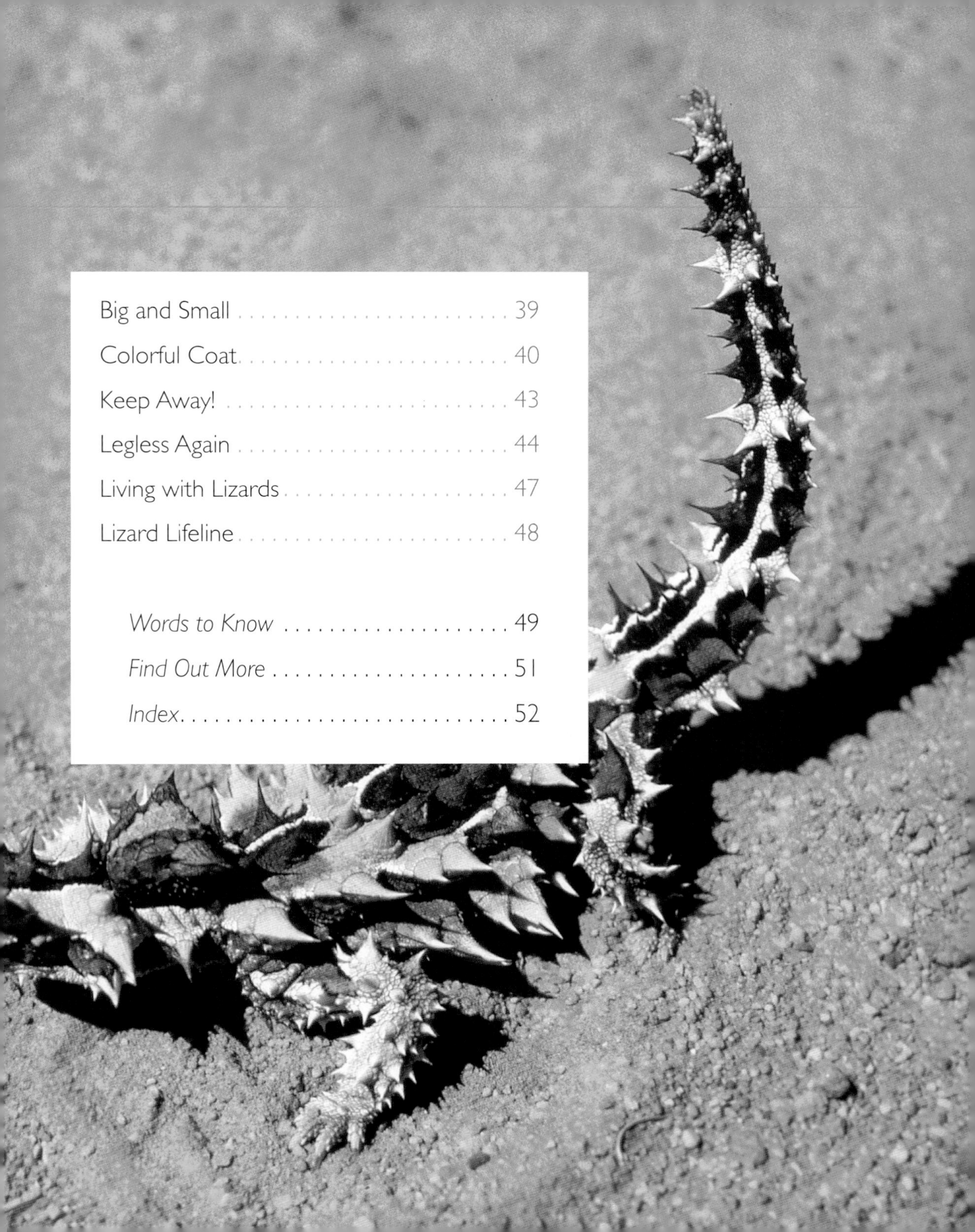

# FACT FILE: Lizards

| | |
|---|---|
| **Class** | Reptiles (Reptilia) |
| **Order** | Snakes and lizards (Squamata) |
| **Families** | Worldwide, there are about 29 families of lizards, including geckos, skinks, and iguanas |
| **Genera** | About 50 genera in the world |
| **Species** | About 4,600 known species of lizards |
| **World distribution** | All continents, except Antarctica |
| **Habitat** | Everywhere from tropical forests to baking deserts, lush meadows to rock beaches |
| **Distinctive physical characteristics** | A long body and tail covered with scales; most have four legs and eyelids that can blink |
| **Habits** | Lizards rely on the Sun's warmth for body heat so they often spend time basking; in very warm places lizards might be active at night |
| **Diet** | Most lizards eat small animals; some hunt larger animals; a few are plant eaters |

# Introduction

Do you ever think you've seen a lizard only to find that when you look again you are staring at an empty rock or wall? Chances are the lizard was there. But in the blink of an eye it disappeared into the nearest crack or tuft of grass. For their size, these shy creatures are among the fastest runners and climbers in the world. But there's a lot more to lizards than that. Let's take a closer look at some of their amazing tricks—from walking upside down and gliding though the air, to changing color before your eyes.

**A giant ground gecko from Africa curls its tail up in the air to warn off a predator.**

Lizards are covered
in scales and have legs
that stick out of the
sides of their body.

# What Is a Lizard?

Lizards are **reptiles**, like snakes, alligators, and turtles. These creatures are **cold-blooded** animals. That means that they can't heat their bodies from the inside like you can.

Most lizards have a long body and a long tail. The tail might be thin or very fat. The majority of lizards have short legs that stick out from the sides. Other four-legged animals' legs are below their body. However, there are several types of lizards that don't have any legs at all.

Among the reptiles, the lizards' closest relatives are the snakes. Both snakes and lizards have skin covered in **scales**. The Latin word *squama* means "scale," and so scientists call snakes and lizards Squamata (SKWA-MA-TA).

# Grandpa Dinosaur

Reptiles were the first animals with a backbone to live their whole life on land without having to go back into water to breed. They have been around for about 330 million years. The first reptiles looked somewhat like salamanders and laid their eggs on land. The first lizards came along later—about 180 million years ago.

Lizards belong to the same large group as the dinosaurs. The word *dinosaur* is Latin for "terrible lizard." The dinosaurs were the biggest animals on Earth for millions of years. But dinosaurs died out about 65 million years ago, leaving some of their relatives behind. These surviving dino-relatives are the crocodiles, snakes, lizards, and birds. Some scientists think the **ancestor** of all birds is a tree-climbing lizardlike reptile with feathers instead of scales!

Mammals, such as mice, dogs, monkeys, and people, have reptile ancestors, too. They belonged to a different group of reptiles called the therapsids.

This fossilized lizard lived in the Jurassic period, 248 to 208 million years ago.

9

Crocodiles—which are not lizards—are bigger and more dangerous than lizards.

# Lizard Look-alikes

Some animals look a lot like lizards. Those include other types of reptiles such as crocodiles. Some nonreptiles, such as salamanders, look a lot like lizards, too.

Crocodiles have a similar body shape to some lizards. But crocodiles belong to a different group of reptiles. They are as closely related to birds as they are to lizards and snakes. The salamanders and newts also have a long body, four short legs, and a long tail, just like most lizards. But their slimy skin has no scales. Salamanders are not reptiles but **amphibians**. Salamanders cannot stray far from water without drying out.

Snakes are similar to some legless lizards, such as slowworms. But unlike lizards snakes do not have eyes that can blink or obvious ear openings.

# Lizards of the World

Most of the world's lizards live in hot tropical countries. There, lizards never have any trouble keeping warm. Some lizards manage to survive in cooler places. But in winter these lizards hide away in burrows and **hibernate**, or sleep, until spring.

In all these different countries, lizards live in a huge variety of habitats, or types of places. Many are forest dwellers. Some forest lizards live on the ground and others scramble about in the trees. Other lizards live in deserts. There, the lizards have to hide away most of the day to avoid overheating or drying out in the baking sun. The best chance of seeing a lizard is in a grassland. There, it is warm during the day and cool at night. In the morning, lizards come out in the open and sunbathe to warm up.

This thorny devil, a type of spiky lizard, lives in the deserts of Australia.

Some lizards, such as
this gecko, have a see-
through scale called a
brille that covers and
protects their eyes.

# Scaly Skin

The scales that cover a lizard's body are small flat disks made of a substance called **keratin**. Scales grow from the lizard's skin the way hair grows from your head and nails grow from your fingers and toes. In fact, hair and nails are made of keratin, too.

In some lizards, the scales overlap to make a tough covering that protects the skin from all sorts of damage. The scales of the monitor lizards look like mosaic tiles. In others, such as the speedy racerunners, the scales are so tiny they look like glitter. They give the lizard the freedom of movement it needs to run fast.

Some lizards, such as night lizards and geckos, have a special clear scale over each eye. This scale is called a **brille**, or spectacle. Brilles protect the eyes from being damaged by dirt and debris.

# Starting Out

Lizards hatch from eggs. The eggs have shells that are soft and rubbery, not hard and brittle like birds' eggs. Female lizards choose a damp, sheltered place to lay their eggs. There, the eggs are hidden from view, do not dry out, and are neither too hot nor too cold. For some types of lizards, it is difficult to find a safe place to lay eggs. Therefore, the females of these lizards keep the eggs inside their body. The young hatch inside their mother and are born soon after.

When baby lizards are ready to hatch, they make a tear in the eggshell using a special sharp tooth on their snout called an egg tooth. Then, the young scramble out. Sometimes they eat the eggshell. Baby lizards are on their own from the start. Their parents do not look after them. They have to fend for themselves.

The sand lizard's eggshells are soft, unlike birds' eggs.

Some female lizards, such as this whiptail, can have babies without mating with a male lizard.

# Amazing Births

Some female lizards produce young all by themselves, without having to **mate** with a male. That usually happens when there are no males around. For example, a female lizard might be washed up on an island where no other lizards live. Scientists call this way of breeding **parthenogenesis** (PAR-THU-NO-JE-NUH-SUS). Geckos, whiptails, and Komodo dragons can produce young by this process. Their young lizards might be male or female. This allows a species, or type, of lizard to get settled in a new place or recover from very small numbers.

# Lizard Senses

Most lizards have good eyesight. But they are better at seeing moving objects than still ones. If you want to sneak up on a lizard, you have to do it very slowly! In a few lizards, such as burrowing blind lizards, the eyes are completely covered with skin. Chameleons have strange eyes. The part of the eye sticking out of the socket is cone-shaped, or conical. The eyes swivel in their sockets and can point in different directions at the same time!

Lizards that do not see so well make up for their poor sight with fantastic senses of smell and taste. They use their nose for smelling and also have an extra smelling organ in the mouth. When you see a lizard flicking its tongue in and out, the reptile is collecting and tasting chemicals in the air.

Many lizards also have sharp hearing. You can sometimes see their ear openings at the back of the head, behind the eyes.

Chameleons can rotate and focus each eye separately, which helps them look for prey and predators.

A panther chameleon flicks out its very long, sticky tongue to catch its dinner.

# Making a Meal

Most lizards eat small animals such as spiders, worms, beetles, ants, and centipedes. Lizards are not too fussy. Any small bug that makes a false move is snapped up and swallowed whole.

Speed is the key for most hungry lizards. The slow-moving chameleon has a tongue that is sticky and stretchy and can be longer than the rest of its body! The tongue is kept rolled up inside the mouth. The chameleon can flick out its tongue to slurp up an unsuspecting insect in an instant.

Larger lizards usually have a bigger appetite. Monitor lizards catch and eat other lizards and small mammals. While the largest lizard of all, the Komodo dragon, sometimes kills wild pigs or even sheep.

Not all lizards are hunters. The marine iguanas look fierce, but their favorite food is seaweed!

# Energy Savers

Many lizards do not eat very much at all. Some lizards can go for weeks or months without a meal. How do they manage to do that without starving? Warm-blooded animals, such as mammals and birds, use a lot of energy keeping their body running at a constant temperature. Just like heating a house, keeping a body warm uses fuel. Our fuel is food. Your body burns food in much the same way that a fire burns wood or coal. Lizards and other reptiles are cold-blooded. Since they do not have to maintain a constant temperature, they need less energy to survive. So they can manage on very little food.

# Sun Worshippers

Lizards use energy directly from the Sun to warm up their body. That is why you often see lizards lying in a sunny spot, soaking up the warmth. Some lizards flatten their body so as much skin as possible is exposed to the Sun's rays. Other lizards change to a darker color when they are sunbathing. Dark colors absorb more sunlight—and more heat—than light colors.

Some lizards have special frills of skin around their neck that act as sun catchers. Blood passing through the frills is heated by the Sun. This warm blood in turn heats the whole lizard as it flows around the body. On a sunny day a sluggish frilled lizard is soon warmed up and running around.

A desert iguana
warms itself
by basking in
the sunshine.

# Taking to the Air

Some lizards are great leapers. In Africa, the blue-tailed tree lizard has large scales on its feet and tail. These scales help keep the lizard stable when it leaps from tree to tree.

A few lizards have taken leaping one step further and turned it into gliding! The flying geckos of Southeast Asia have webbed toes and a big flap of skin along both sides of the body. When flying geckos leap, they spread their legs. The flaps open like the wings of a hang glider or a microlight plane. The flying draco is even more impressive. It glides on a pair of "wings" that are supported by extra-long ribs. The flying draco can glide 165 feet (50 m) or more!

A flying draco
glides effortlessly
between trees.

A collared lizard dashes away on its back legs.

# Speed Stars

Many lizards are fast runners. The racehorse goanna, a monitor lizard from Australia, can run at about 16 miles per hour (25 km/h). This lizard is 5 feet (1.5 m) long. The six-lined racerunner from the southern United States is faster still at 18 miles per hour (29 km/h). That is despite being only about 8 inches (22 cm) long!

Another Australian species, the lashtail, reaches 15 miles per hour (22 km/h) on just two legs! The basilisk lizards of South America use the same two-legged style to sprint across the surface of pools of water. The basilisks' back feet act like paddles. Their feet slap the surface of the water so hard that the lizard does not sink.

# Fancy Footwork

When it comes to fancy footwork, geckos are hard to beat. They can run up smooth walls or windows. Some can even hang out upside down on a ceiling. Their feet stick to smooth surfaces like glue. But puzzlingly, there is no glue. A gecko is able to "unstick" itself whenever it wants. It took scientists a very long time to figure out how the lizards manage this feat.

The pads on a gecko's toes are covered with millions of tiny hairs. A powerful microscope is needed to see these hairs. The hairs are so small they can stick to a wall the same way dust settles on a vertical surface, using tiny electrical forces. When the gecko wants to move, it curls its toes up and peels the hairs off the wall—a bit like unpeeling sticky tape.

This common house
gecko has no problem
walking up walls.

Marine iguanas are
excellent swimmers.

# Sea Dragons

Most lizards spend their whole life on land.
But a few have returned to the water. The
magnificent marine iguanas of the Galápagos
Islands, off South America, spend half their
time in the sea. They eat seaweed, which they
collect from the seabed 50 feet (16 m) down.
Their long, flat tail acts as a paddle. Their
long, curved claws latch onto rocks on the
seabed while they collect seaweed. The iguanas
have to be very tough. Most of the seaweed they
love grows in the surf zone. This means the
iguanas have to put up with being tumbled
about by the waves. When the iguanas have
had enough, they scramble out onto the rocky
beaches to rest and warm up in the sun.

# Detachable Tail

Occasionally, even the fastest and best-disguised lizards find themselves getting caught by an even quicker **predator**. But that doesn't always mean the end. Many lizards have an amazing ability to simply drop their tail. Scientists call this process **autotomy**, which means "self-cutting." Often the tail keeps wriggling, so the predator does not realize the rest of its meal is getting away!

The lost tail grows back, but it often looks different from the original tail. Many lizards have a brightly colored tail that seems to attract attention. The rest of the body is camouflaged. That means predators tend to go for the tail rather than the head or body, which the lizard cannot afford to lose! Some lizards lose their tail many times in their lifetime. But the loss does not seem to do the lizards any real harm.

A moorish gecko has shed its tail. A predator might eat the twitching tail, while the lizard makes its getaway.

**Komodo dragons, the biggest living lizards, live on a handful of islands in Indonesia.**

# Big and Small

Do you believe in dragons? Don't listen to anyone who tells you they don't exist. We're not talking the flying, fire-breathing kind of dragon but the real, live lizard kind. The largest lizards are Komodo dragons, which grow up to 10 feet (3 m) long and weigh up to 200 pounds (90 kg). They come from Indonesia.

At the other end of the scale, the world's smallest reptile is a lizard. There are two species of dwarf geckos from the Caribbean that grow to a little over half an inch (1.9 cm) long. These tiny lizards are small enough to curl up on your thumbnail!

# Colorful Coat

Camouflage means using colors and patterns to hide against a background. Many lizards are brilliant at camouflaging themselves. Most lizards are colored to match the background they live in. Many lizards have patterns that make their disguise even more convincing.

The most amazing colors are seen on the chameleons. They are famous for being able to change color to match their background or to suit their mood. Being difficult to see has two big advantages: Chameleons can sneak up on **prey** such as insects, but avoid being spotted by bigger predators. At other times, chameleons want to be seen. For example, males might flush red, yellow, purple, and blue to impress females or to drive off rival males.

A chameleon makes itself green to blend in with the leaves of the shrub in which it sits waiting for insects.

A frilled lizard uses its frilly collar to make itself look big and scary to other animals.

# Keep Away!

Many lizards are great bluffers. Some legless Australian lizards have the same coloring as poisonous brown snakes that live in the same place. If the lizards are threatened they rear up and puff up their neck, just like the brown snake does.

Other lizards try to bluff their way out of trouble by making themselves look much bigger or more dangerous than they really are. The frilled lizard is a great bluffer. It has an enormous frill around its neck, which usually lies folded out of sight. But as soon as the lizard feels threatened, the frill opens like an umbrella. It's enough to make most predators think twice.

The American horned lizards have very strange ways of avoiding unwanted attention. They can squirt blood from their eyes! Not surprisingly, predators find that threatening and they back off.

# Legless Again

Some lizards look more like snakes because they have no legs. They are called slowworms and glass snakes. At some point in the past, their ancestors lost their legs and found they could survive even better without them. Legless lizards grow up to 3 feet (90 cm) long.

Slowworms and glass snakes move by wriggling along the ground like a snake. Their scales need to be tough to protect the body. These tough scales are very smooth and shiny. Like many other lizards, slowworms and glass snakes drop their tails when attacked. In fact, even gentle handling can make these lizards "break off" their tail. That's why they are called glass snakes!

A slowworm isn't a
worm or a snake—
it's a legless lizard!

The Gila monster, found in the deserts of North America, has a venomous bite.

# Living with Lizards

Many people living in warm parts of the world
are used to seeing lizards close to home. In some
places, lizards even come into houses. Geckos
are commonly found in houses, where they do
a useful job eating flies and spiders.

But not all lizards are as nice to have around.
There are two species of poisonous lizards—the
Gila (HEE-LA) monster and the Mexican beaded
dragon. A bite from one of these two might not
kill you, but it would make you very ill. Both
Gilas and Mexican beaded lizards have poison
glands in their cheeks. When the lizards bite,
**venom** from the gland seeps in among the teeth
and leaks into the wound.

# Lizard Lifeline

About 200 of the world's lizard species are
in danger of becoming **extinct**, or dying out.
In fact, half a dozen or more seem to have
disappeared completely since they were first
discovered. The rarest lizard in the world is the
blue iguana from the Cayman Islands in the
Caribbean. They could be extinct within 10
years. The main reason why extinctions occur
is because the animal's habitat is destroyed.

The sad truth is that many more lizards may
be in danger of extinction, too. Lizards do not
normally attract the same attention as some other
groups of animals, such as birds and mammals.
Perhaps because they can be difficult to see in
the wild people tend to forget they are there.
But as you have discovered in this book, lizards
are fascinating animals. They deserve far more
attention from scientists and other people working
to protect the habitats of wild plants and animals.

# Words to Know

**Amphibians**   A group of animals that lives both on land and in water. Frogs, toads, and salamanders are amphibians.

**Ancestors**   Animals that lived a long time ago and from which today's animals are descended.

**Autotomy**   The process by which a lizard drops its tail to avoid being caught.

**Brille**   A clear scale over the eyes of snakes and some lizards. Also called a spectacle.

**Cold-blooded**   Having no internal control of body temperature. Lizards are cold-blooded.

**Extinct**   When all of a certain type of animal are dead and gone forever.

**Hibernate**   To go into a long, deep winter sleep.

| | |
|---|---|
| **Keratin** | The substance that makes up hair, horns, nails, feathers, and scales. Keratin is a type of protein. |
| **Mate** | To come together to produce young. |
| **Partheno-genesis** | When a female animal produces young without mating with a male. |
| **Predator** | An animal that kills and eats other animals. |
| **Prey** | An animal that is hunted for food by another animal, the predator. |
| **Reptiles** | A group of cold-blooded animals that includes snakes, alligators, turtles, dinosaurs, and lizards. |
| **Scales** | Small tough, overlapping plates that grow on the skin of lizards and other reptiles and on the legs of birds. |
| **Venom** | A poisonous substance produced by some animals. |

# Find Out More

Books

Badger, D. *Lizards: A Natural History of Some Uncommon Creatures: Extraordinary Chameleons, Iguanas, Geckos, and More*. St. Paul, Minnesota: Voyageur Press, 2006.

Mattison, Chris. *Lizards of the World*. New York: Facts On File, 2004.

Web sites

**Lizards**
*www.enchantedlearning.com/subjects/reptiles/lizard/ Lizardprintout.shtml*
Printouts to color in and facts about many lizards.

**Marine iguanas**
*www.geo.cornell.edu/geology/GalapagosWWW/ MarineIguanas.html*
Information and pictures of marine iguanas.

# Index